AF586505

DON'T Get a coach until you've read this

A book from Producing Possibility

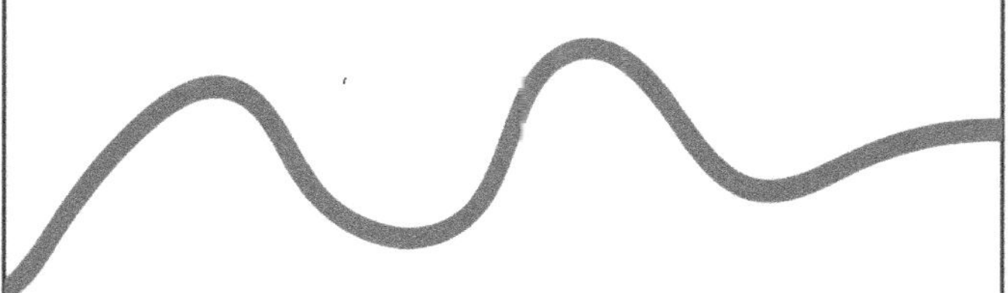

DON'T Get a coach until you've read this

Get the most out of coaching
with some simp e preparation

Rob Michael PhD

Don't Get a Coach Until You've Read This

First published 2024 by Producing Possibility Ltd

ISBN 978-1-0685248-0-6

A CIP catalogue record for this book is available from the British Library.

A book from Producing Possibility
producingpossibility.uk

DON'T GET A COACH until you know...

The WHY

Clarifying what you want and how coaching can help

The WHO

Selecting a coach who's going to be right for you

Don't get a coach ... ?!

"Don't get a coach? That's a good one, coming from a coach!"

I get it – it's perhaps an odd title for a book written by someone who loves coaching and has benefited so much from it personally. But hear me out – I'm only asking that you get clear on two things before you start with a coach. I'll explain why briefly, and then we can get into the meat of the book.

Coaching is a big deal today - and with good reason. Worldwide, professional, sports and life coaching is growing all the time. We're more interested than ever before in improving our lives and our work, and coaching can be massively helpful.

The bad news, though, is that coaching is often not as impactful as we'd hope. And that means some people invest their time, effort and money into getting a coach but don't get the benefit they could. You may even have met some people who've had that experience or read posts warning you not to bother. I'm a coach but I'm here to tell you people are right to sound a note of caution for anyone considering getting a coach. This isn't 'fake news' – not every coaching engagement or programme delivers what the client needed.

The good news is we know what works and how to avoid disappointment and waste. The bottom line for most people is to get things right before you even start with a coach – it's the foundations that make the biggest difference to the success of your coaching. That's confirmed by extensive evidence and my own personal experience, having seen coaching from every angle.

This short book aims to help you ask the right questions before you even have your first session of coaching. It won't take long to read, but you'll be glad you bothered.

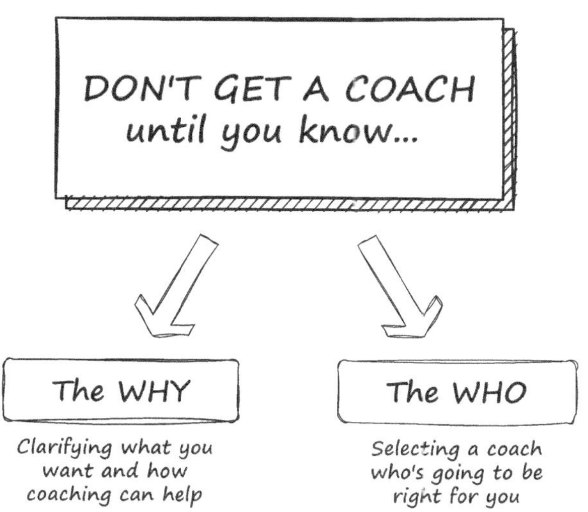

Make notes !

You can use this book however you like. As it's intended as a practical guide rather than a textbook, I'd suggest reading it with a pen at the ready. There are plenty of spaces for your own notes, and I've included prompts and questions.

Treating this as a workbook should give you the most benefit.

There are spaces in the book for your notes, or you can download a worksheet free online.

dontgetacoach.com/notes

Once you've got a coach and begun working with them, you'll want to look back at your notes, to see how you're achieving what you initially set out to.

Who is coaching for?

You may have an image of the kind of person who works with a coach. There are plenty of stereotypes around. Perhaps it's for senior executives who meet their coach in a glitzy glass-walled office? Perhaps it's for media types, lounging in their magazine-ready mansion? Perhaps it's for high-flying professionals, eager to shine now they've reached the top?

Personally, I have worked with all of these types of people - and many more besides. I've seen people from beginners to experts, from the very well-known to the pretty well-hidden all benefit from coaching. Sure, different people have different needs, situations and budgets. But the basic questions of life and work are remarkably similar, I've found.

So who is coaching for? Well - you, me, anyone who wants to see clearer and move forward more confidently. Getting benefits from coaching doesn't depend on your background, your level of education, your wealth, seniority or fame. It DOES require clarity, commitment and chemistry - and we'll deal with all three of those ingredients in this book. But don't assume anyone is excluded from the world of coaching, not least you. The fact that you're reading this in the first place is a strong indication you're likely to get on really well with coaching.

> Tom is an engineer needing to decide which way to jump when big changes hit his employer.
>
> Asiya is a doctor struggling with continual conflict with two close colleagues.

Rebecca is soon to be married but is worried about how to handle a difficult issue in her fiancé's family.

Jonathan is an experienced lawyer unsure whether to take the opportunity to shift into a new speciality.

Susannah has recently joined the board of a charity but is unsure how to play a useful role.

John is struggling to get different teams at work to collaborate on a major project.

Louise wants to stop feeling so much like an imposter since her promotion at work.

Rob is feeling directionless in his job and wants to find something new and stimulating.

Sue and Mike love each other but want to argue less.

What do these people all have in common? They each say that using coaching was 'very helpful' in getting them where they wanted to be.

If you too want to get a fresh perspective, understand a situation or people better, or grow yourself, then coaching is likely to be useful for you. Later in the book, we'll look in more detail at the specific ways coaching can help in different situations.

All the people and situations mentioned in this book are real, but names and some other details have been altered to protect confidentiality.

About me

I am a coach and consultant based in the UK. In this book I'll share practical tips I've collected as I've looked at coaching from different angles:

- **Personal.** I have had coaching myself at several points of my career and personal life. I've benefitted a lot from it – some times more than others.
- **Professional.** I have provided coaching to clients on four continents from the most diverse backgrounds imaginable. I work with people and teams in the public, private and non-profit sectors, and my clients have ranged from government-level leaders to ghetto kids with potential.
- **Research and development.** I have a background in research and have overseen research into career development, burnout and performance improvement.
- **Funder.** I have commissioned professional coaching programmes costing millions of pounds in the UK.

All these perspectives have convinced me of one thing – getting the foundations right is crucial if you're to get the most out of your experience with coaching. This book aims to help you with the two big foundational questions at the start: WHY are you looking at coaching and WHO is going to best for you?

Whether you're considering getting a coach for personal or professional reasons - or a bit of both - this book should help you get the most out of it.

Part 1: The WHY

DON'T GET A COACH
until you know...

The WHY

Clarifying what you want and how coaching can help

The WHO

Selecting a coach who's going to be right for you

Having clarity about WHY you want coaching is the biggest thing that will determine how much benefit you get from it.

The WHY

Clarifying what you want and how coaching can help

WHY? It's the question kids ask which can stress out parents the most - worse even than "are we there yet?". And for many parents it's a huge sigh of relief when our kids grow out of it asking why every other minute. Yet for many adults it's a question we don't give enough time to.

So I'll ask again - WHY?

Why are you looking into coaching? It might not be the question your friends would go to first. It might not be the thing you've spent most time checking out on YouTube. But I promise it's going to be the most important question if you're to get this right.

Getting clarity about the reasons you want coaching will:

- save you time
- guide your choice of coaching programme
- help you select the right kind of coach
- make it less likely you'll discover too late that it's not actually coaching you want (which happens more often than you might think)

Most of us are fairly well-prepared for basic questions about why we're doing something. How else would we get what we want at the Post Office counter or the doctor's? "How can I help?" means "why are you here?". And our reply is usually a straightforward affair - "I need to send this parcel", or "my knee's still hurting". There are always times when we're not quite so clear about why we've come, or we can't fully remember, but we generally muddle through OK.

Coaching is different. There are several reasons:

- coaching can help with an even wider range of needs than a good Post Office
- there are even more different types of coach than types of doctor
- coaching is going to require a way more active contribution from you than almost anything else you've ever bought

Having clarity about why you're looking for a coach will help you get more benefit more quickly, and save the all-too-embarrassing moment a coach has to say "I'm afraid that's not what I'm here for". Which often doesn't come until you've had two or three paid sessions!

Thankfully it's not essential to spend too long on the question of why. Your coach, like your doctor, isn't going to need you to come with everything completely sorted out. But it's surprising how many coachees are surprised to be asked why they've come, and it's sad when they don't get all the potential benefit as a result.

WHY can be something people get stuck with, so I've found it helpful to break it down into 3 simpler questions:

- **where** am I now?
- **where** do I want to be?
- **how** do I think coaching can help?

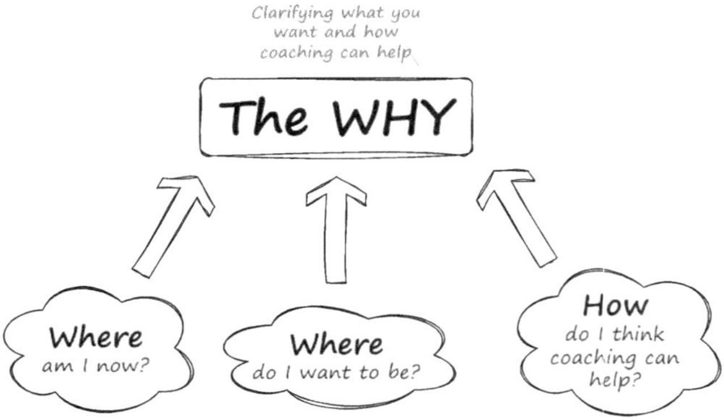

Clarifying what you want and how coaching can help

The WHY

Where am I now?

Where do I want to be?

How do I think coaching can help?

Where am I now?

Where am I? What's the situation? What's occurring? What's up?

However you phrase it, being clear in your own mind about where you are now is a helpful first step in getting what you want out of coaching. You and your coach are going to need a basic shared understanding of the good, the bad and the ugly of the situation you're in at the moment. Are you interested in coaching because the current situation is simply unbearable? Have you reached the point where you just can't ignore an issue? Or is the situation more 'meh' and you want to explore possible changes to remove some niggles? Or perhaps you're actually in a good place right now and you're wanting to explore potential changes for different reasons.

Being ready to talk with your coach about the current situation you're in is helpful partly because it can be a quick way to build a rapport together. Even more, though, it helps to guide what you work on together.

Why not pause for a moment now and jot down answers to these questions for yourself:

What do I want my coaching to focus on?

What are the good and bad aspects of my current situation?

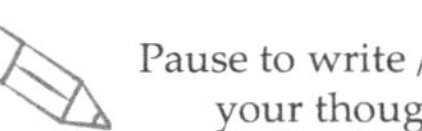

Where do I want to be?

Whether your current situation is good, bad or indifferent, it's good to get some clarity about where you would like to go with coaching.

I don't believe you should get too hung up on whether you're being ambitious enough or practical enough when thinking about your goals with coaching. Not yet anyway. We all differ in our natural tendencies and strengths. Some of us find it quite easy to dream big / think outside the box / do blue-sky thinking ... or whatever the current buzz phrase is. We can get into lots of detail about exactly how a completely different future could look for us, how it would work and feel. If that's you, your ability to envision different possibilities is going to be a real asset in coaching.

On the other hand, some of us find it really hard to map out an imaginative new future for ourselves. Letting go of the practical considerations, the 'art of the possible' and the reality of where we are right now can seem unreal, unattractive or unattainable. If that's you, your practical mindset is going be a real asset in coaching.

How will I know my coaching has been helpful?

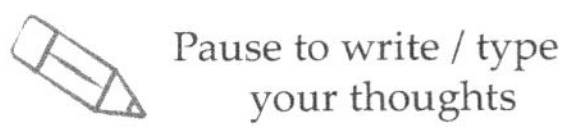

How can coaching help?

> *"[coaching is] unlocking a person's potential to maximize their own performance. It is helping them to learn rather than teaching them" (John Whitmore[1])*

There are good reasons why so many people rave about coaching. It's not a panacea for everything, but there are some things it's almost uniquely good at.

Coaching can help with a huge number of things, so I've listed them below but then grouped them into 4 main types of situation – sensemaking, planning, accountability and performance.

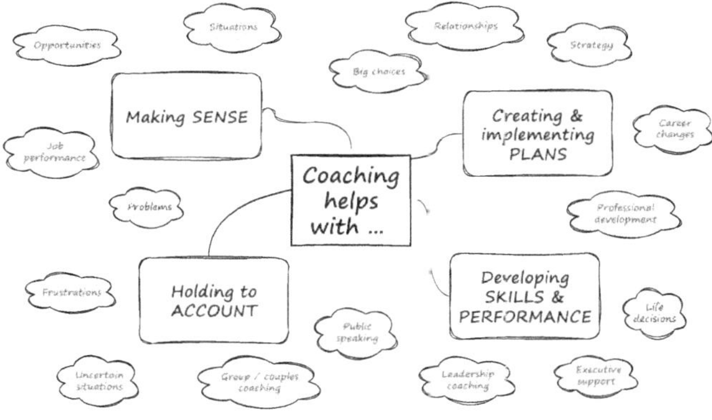

[1] Whitmore, J. (2017) *Coaching for performance: the principles and practice of coaching and leadership.* London: Nicholas Brealey Publishing. ISBN 978-1-4736-5812-7

a) Making sense of situations, people & problems

Often the most impactful thing about coaching is that it helps you to see things differently. This can be key to creating plans for action, working through complex problems or growing in your effectiveness. Your coach will help you to gain clarity and new perspectives on your current situation, your behaviours and your skills. Sometimes, gaining a better perspective on things is actually the biggest key to success. It's the most-cited benefit which my clients mention after our work together, being mentioned explicitly by nearly 90% of people in their feedback.

One of the key ways that coaching helps people make sense of situations is by fostering a deeper understanding of their own thoughts, emotions, and behaviours. Often, individuals face challenges or confusion because they are unable to see the broader picture or identify the underlying causes of their struggles. These are things it's often difficult to see objectively - as Les Brown has said "you can't see the picture when you're in the frame". A coach brings skilled questioning to help clients explore their situations, experiences and perceptions. This process can lead to significant insights, as clients often uncover patterns or beliefs that were previously hidden or unexamined.

As well as helping clients understand their own internal processes, coaching also aids in making sense of interpersonal relationships and dynamics. Whether in a professional setting or personal life, understanding how to effectively interact with others is crucial. Coaches assist clients in developing emotional intelligence, which includes the ability to recognize and manage one's own emotions, as well as the capacity to understand and influence the emotions of others. Through role-playing, feedback, and reflective exercises, clients learn to navigate conflicts, build stronger relationships, and communicate more effectively.

Crucially, coaching creates a safe, non-judgmental space where you can explore your situation, thoughts and feelings without fear of criticism or gossip. Coaches use empathetic listening and validation to create this supportive atmosphere, which in turn fosters greater self-awareness and self-acceptance in clients. Sometimes it will involve stepping back to see 'the bigger picture' or appreciate new perspectives, other times you'll dig down into the details of an issue. Either way, effective coaching almost always results in us seeing and understanding things better, so we can achieve what we want.

Shaheena was a manager who had recently taken on a new team whose performance was poor. Her first three months had been full of frustrating failed attempts to get them to work harder. She engaged me as a coach to help her find creative new solutions to improve their performance. As we talked through different aspects of the team's performance and her failed improvement efforts, I asked if she thought every person was clear about the responsibilities and boundaries for their role.

The question was clearly a surprise. The organisation as a whole had a strong focus on outcomes and pace towards targets, and teams were reorganised quite frequently. This had become a normal feature of life for Shaheena, who had navigated multiple changes and risen through the ranks of management. However, it transpired that she herself wasn't entirely clear on how this team's targets related to each person in it, and she agreed that they might not be clear either about what exactly their own responsibilities and boundaries were.

Shaheena had got to where she was partly because of her own comfort with ambiguity and a willingness to be both flexible and thick-skinned when working with others. Stepping back, though, she was able to see that her team might be struggling to impress because they weren't sure what they were meant to be doing. With this new perspective, she decided to put her plans to one side and spend time enquiring about how the team saw their roles and ways of working together.

This immediately confirmed that there was little clarity and limited confidence to take responsibility without that. It also demonstrated that simply asking questions about the issue began to build people's confidence to tell her details about the specific issues which hadn't come to light before. In just two months, Shaheena reported that the team's performance and attitude was 'unrecognisable'. There were still a bunch of improvements to make, but they had momentum and a team willing to try new things for the first time.

As a coach, I hadn't given Shaheena any new plans or trained her in new skills. I had just helped her step outside the picture to see her familiar setting from a different perspective.

b) Creating and implementing plans

Coaching can help you make change happen in a more successful and sustainable way. Many people use coaching to help them create and implement plans for getting something done that matters to them, either in their personal life or at work. Coaching can help you with making better plans, with the process of implementing them or just with the hard slog of keeping going.

In my own work as a leader, I've experienced failure and disappointment on numerous occasions. So many great ideas have failed to deliver great results. How come? Looking back, I can see that a major reason is that I didn't have a great plan to make the great idea a reality. The evidence about personal change and professional change leadership confirms that I'm not alone. I once asked a cohort of senior healthcare leaders how many of their good ideas were delivering results a year later. They estimated it was less than 5% - 19 out of 20 of these intelligent people's inspirations went nowhere. I find that remarkable, depressing and motivating all at the same time. What a huge number! What a terrible waste! But what a motivation for me to promote coaching as a means to ensure we have great plans for our great ideas.

Maybe you've started off with a really great plan and you still haven't achieved great results. Often this is because we forget to check regularly that the plan is working as intended. Your plan may have been great, but no plan is perfect – and we should be ready to adapt as we go along. The armed forces say that 'no plan survives contact with the enemy' – there's always a need to adapt once we've begun implementing a plan. They have disciplines in place to review and revise plans continually – and they do it as a team, coaching one another. Any one of us can have a fantastic *idea*, but a really successful *plan* is usually a team effort. The spark of inspiration can be instantaneous but developing a great plan is a process that can take a lot of time. Working with a coach to monitor and learn from the process of implementing your plan can really help in improving success.

Lastly, another major reason we can be disappointed or discouraged when we've made a plan is that putting it into action is just plain hard. Do you make New Year resolutions? How many of them do you deliver on? Be honest - are you still going at the halfway point of the year? Research shows that a quarter of us don't make it past the first week of the new year, and only 46% make it through the first 6 months[2]. One of the proven factors to improve our changes is simply having people cheering us on. Talking regularly with a trusted supporter can make all the difference in keeping our energy up.

Mark came to coaching for help with planning a change programme at work. He'd recently been promoted to a director position and was now responsible for simultaneously improving performance and amalgamating two different departments, all while seeing to day-to-day firefighting. When we first met he said his main reason for booking coaching was "just to get some space to think".

Having that space was definitely a major benefit for him. After our first two sessions Mark rated his satisfaction with his situation had improved from 2

---

[2] *New year, New Me: The Science Behind New Year's Resolutions.* Available at: https://blog.experiencepoint.com/2022-new-year-new-me-why-new-years-resolutions-fail

out of 10, to 7. He reported feeling more prepared to lead the programme, and that the main reason was that he'd had the chance to talk through it without distractions, interruptions or "other people's agendas".

Every time he'd tried to sound out a colleague about his plans the conversation had got waylaid by an interruption or strayed into talk about the other person's directorate or corporate goings-on more generally. Coaching was providing a protected, focused time to work on just one thing, and that was clearly helping.

Over the course of 5 coaching sessions, Mark made great strides in developing plans for his change programme, and began implementing them. As we finished his satisfaction with his situation was 9 out of 10, and he said the two main benefits of coaching had been "I can see the wood for the trees at last, and I've now got a really robust programme plan for the next year or two".

c) Holding you to account

Can you remember a really great evening with friends when life is good and you've been relaxed enough to start dreaming out loud? Sharing ideas, spitballing plans? It feels like anything is possible. In those conversations we often drill down to what really matters to us and what we'd love to achieve if only we weren't so busy doing things that matter less. It's brilliant isn't it?

But how many of those 'if only' conversations lead to action? How many of those possibilities have you ever realised? For most of us, the answer is few or none. Have you ever wondered why? It's easy to dismiss these conversations afterwards as being just a 'thing of the moment' or, for some of us, 'the drink talking'. That may be true sometimes - but is it always the case that those ideas and plans are best forgotten?

One thing that's almost always missing is accountability. Friends encourage us to dream - which usually means 'focus on things that matter more than the mundane'. Friends will often take our dreams more seriously than we do, and those conversations may produce some pretty credible plans. But how often do friends then enquire about your progress? How often do you ask a friend what steps they've taken with that plan?

This is another huge benefit of coaching - your coach will help you hold yourself to account for doing more than just talking or planning. A programme of coaching will usually run over several months, specifically so that you can take action and then discuss how it's going. It's not always a comfortable thing, but in my experience, it is always productive. Sometimes it's one of the most impactful aspects of coaching, having someone who will cut through the pleasantries and generalities of a nice chat, and ask 'so how's it going with those things you said you'd do?'.

Accountability is the one ingredient missing from many excellent resolutions and plans. Take something like resolving to lose weight or stop smoking. Extensive research show that you need will (your desire or determination to make a change), practical plans (when exactly are you going to go for a run?) AND accountability. If you miss any one of these, it's way less likely that you'll succeed. And the researchers do mean 'accountability' rather than 'encouragement'. It's nice to have encouragement from friends and family, but it's only when that's linked to *action* that it really contributes to our success. We need will, plans AND accountability to see our resolutions realised.

Ideas + Plan + Accountability = SUCCESS

Don't miss this out !

This is where coaching differs from other personal or professional development such as study, conferences or training courses. Not only will your coaching be 100% tailored to your specific needs, it will support - even nudge - you into action. Given that many of us learn best through doing, this also means you may learn more from coaching too.

Suzanne sought coaching because she wasn't coping with her workload and, in her words, 'had zero work-life balance'. Her senior management role in the NHS was typically demanding 55-60 hours a week from her. It wasn't unusual for her to work every day for two or three weeks in a row, and she always took her laptop on holiday. Having done this for 5 unrelenting years, the strain was clearly showing - Suzanne wasn't sleeping well, she had almost no quality time with family or friends, and had all but stopped cycling - her biggest source of relaxation. Now she felt that she was underperforming at work and was too often snappy with her team, some of whom had commented that she seemed always distracted.

As we began discussing potential solutions to her situation, it was clear that Suzanne had no lack of ideas. In just 5 minutes of brainstorming she surprised me by listing 18 specific actions that we both thought seemed promising. Then came the next surprise - looking back through the list she'd just made, she told me that she'd had every one of these thoughts before. In fact she could recall chatting about at least half of them with friends or colleagues in the past.

So what had gone wrong? Why was she still overwhelmed, underperforming and desperate? Accountability. As we picked two or three ideas to explore, Suzanne recollected how she'd been encouraged to have had the idea in the first place, and had listed practical actions she could take. She'd shared these with other people, who had empathised with her situation and encouraged her that she seemed to have a good plan. But there was no accountability in place - she didn't have any conversations with those people later on where they asked how it was going. Perhaps they assumed things were going OK now, perhaps they'd forgotten the previous conversation - who knows? But the encouragement about her ideas and plans hadn't led anywhere. The accountability ingredient was missing.

So we picked two ideas Suzanne felt particularly positive about, planned out actions she could take - and then, crucially, scheduled our next meeting for 2 weeks to check in on progress. At that meeting we got straight into an accountability conversation. She reported what actions she'd taken and how they had worked out. I probed about the actions she hadn't mentioned and we uncovered the reasons behind those failures. We brainstormed ideas for solutions to some pervasive blockers she faced, updated the action plans - and scheduled to meet again in 2 weeks.

We repeated this cycle several times. Each meeting went a little better than the last. Suzanne got used to facing up honestly to the reality of how she was putting her plans into action. She got better at spotting the thoughts and habits that kept holding her back, and - crucially - started holding herself to account. When she reached the point of being confident to do that alone, we agreed our work together could end.

As agreed, I contacted Suzanne three months after our last session. Her fulsome reply was hugely encouraging. She'd implemented 11 practical changes, she was feeling 'at least 50% more on top of work', was spending more quality time with herself and friends, and was actually putting in fewer hours per week.

How did this coaching programme help Suzanne? She'd been stuck in this situation for a number of years and had tried and failed several times to fix it. The ideas were the same. The plans were quite similar. But this time, coaching had added the accountability ingredient - and, hey presto, her life and work were significantly better.

As part of the regular check-ins you schedule with your coach, they will ask if you've done the things you said you would. They'll help you evaluate your actions and their impact, assess how the plan is working, and make sense of lessons you can take from the journey so far. It's not necessarily a comfortable thing, being asked "so how's it gone since last time". In fact, I've had more than one client say they came to a session with a degree of dread about it. But I've also had many say it was THE most impactful aspect of having coaching. Being held to account for taking action, implementing our plans and learning as we go - it can totally change a nice idea into a success story.

How will it help me to be held to account by a coach?

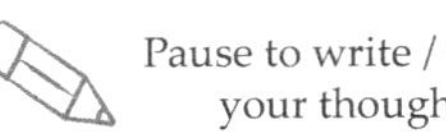

d) Developing skills and improving performance

Coaching is proven to help people learn new skills and improve existing ones. There's actually strong evidence showing it can be the fastest way to grow skills. That's particularly true for skills to do with relationships, communication, influencing and leadership[3]. Coaching tends to develop both your knowledge and the ability to apply that knowledge in the real world. That's why it has also been found often to create the deepest learning and the longest-lasting benefits.

Going on training courses, reading books and watching videos are popular and familiar ways of developing your personal or professional skills. The important difference about coaching is that it can be way more personalised to you. Even if you spend hours researching training courses to join or selecting your next book to read, the content is inevitably fixed beforehand. It's either going to try to address a wide range of people or focus on the things the creator is most interested in. There's nothing wrong with that, and there's nothing anyone can do to change it. But it does mean that parts of the course or the book might be completely irrelevant to you, or key issues that matter to you could be covered only briefly or not at all. Coaching, on the other hand, is like a bespoke learning and development programme whose content and pace is led entirely by you. That bespoke and one-to-one aspect is also why it costs more, of course. But with the added benefits, companies who measure these things tend to find the 'return on investment' is so high that coaching is well worth it.

---

[3] Davenport, T.H. (2009) 'Make Better Decisions', Harvard Business Review, 1 November. https://hbr.org/2009/11/make-better-decisions-2

For some skills, a coaching approach might be the only sensible way to grow yourself. For example, athletes improve only a little by increasing their knowledge - the real performance comes through coached practice. In the same way, you can get great ideas about being an effective public speaker by reading a book and watching others - but having a coach support you to apply the theory is where most of the improvement happens.

> Sam came to coaching for help preparing for a big job interview. He was an experienced professional who had been encouraged by colleagues and seniors to apply for a regional management position. He'd already gone through the application for three promising posts but been unsuccessful at the interview stage on each occasion. He was frustrated and puzzled: "why do I keep failing if everyone says I'd be perfect for this kind of role?". The feedback he'd had from the panels had been rather vague. If he was shortlisted this time, he'd have an interview in about four weeks' time. He rated his confidence to do well as 4 out of 10.
>
> Talking with Sam, it was clear he had no lack of enthusiasm or relevant experience for this kind of role. He came across as engaging and authentic. Who wouldn't want to appoint him?
>
> We tried a short mock interview, with me drawing on the job description for ideas about questions in his field. It was immediately obvious, as a third party, where the problem lay. Sam's approach to most questions was to frame the response around individual clients or frontline teams, weaving in issues of strategic leadership but not making them

explicit. The job description of all the posts he'd applied for appeared to major on strategic leadership.

Sam had never been required to speak in a theme-based way under pressure. We agreed to focus on this skill in our work together. Over the course of 4 sessions, Sam practised a number of techniques to help himself step back, see the bigger picture and talk from that perspective, including the client focus within that more strategic framework. We worked on managing time and prioritising ideas to talk about in order not to run out of time or frustrate interviewers.

Sam was shortlisted for interview. He rated his confidence as 9 out of 10, but what we were both looking for was a different outcome from the previous three attempts. He texted me the evening of the interview to say that he'd got the job. Two of the interviewers were actually the same as at his last interview, and when they'd called to offer him the post, one had said "I assume you've had some coaching? You made so much more sense this time."

In the situation I'm focused on, what aspects of my 'performance' (skills / actions / contribution) would I like to improve?

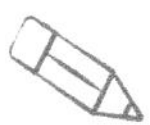

Pause to write / type your thoughts

Mentoring or coaching?

At this point, people often ask about the difference between coaching and mentoring. Are they the same? Are they completely different things? My answer is "yes" and "no" to both. Strictly speaking there are distinctions between them, and there are a great many academic publications exploring this if you're interested. For this book, though, I just want you to have a bit of understanding of the practical differences between them, so you get what's right for you. Too many people are disappointed with coaching because actually it's mentoring they were looking for, but didn't know it.

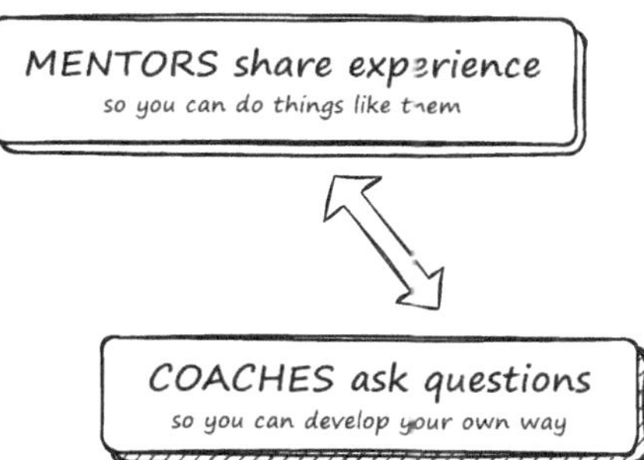

A MENTOR would say...	A COACH would say...
What I would do is...	How could you approach this?
What I did was...	What's the range of options here?
My thinking is...	Let's look at ways to look at this..

Important similarities

Coaching and mentoring are both forms of personal and professional development and are similar in a number of ways. Both offer benefits for individuals, teams and organisations, and they can be useful at various stages of a person's career. They are both more tailored to the specific individual than many other forms of development like training. Both are based around a relationship between the provider of coaching or mentoring (the coach or mentor) and the recipient (coachee or mentee), and can be undertaken one-to-one or in groups. Although both can be used to address performance concerns, for executive and senior staff they are more often used to address a specific challenge, change or growth goal.

Important differences

There are also key differences which you need to know. Sir John Whitmore defined coaching as "unlocking a person's potential to maximize their own performance. It is helping them to learn rather than teaching them"[4]. By contrast, mentoring is more focused on learning from the mentor, from their experience, skills and style. Mentoring is in some ways similar to an apprenticeship model of development - it provides "seasoned counsel and feedback" from "old hands"[5].

---

[4] Whitmore, J. (2017) *Coaching for performance: the principles and practice of coaching and leadership.* ISBN 978-1-4736-5812-7

[5] Janasz, S. de and Peiperl, M. (2015) *CEOs Need Mentors Too.* Harvard Business Review, 1 April 2015. Available at: https://hbr.org/2015/04/ceos-need-mentors-too

Never the twain shall meet?

One way to look at coaching and mentoring is as a spectrum. At one end, mentoring is based around the views and skills of the mentor, and it helps you to become more like them. At the other end, coaching is based around developing your own views and skills, so that you become better at being you. Picture yourself sitting at a potter's wheel - a mentor might put their hands over yours to show how to make a particular shape, whereas a coach would always keep their hands off. Both are trying to help you learn and improve, they're just taking different approaches.

In practice, as with a lot of theoretical spectrums, coaching and mentoring are often blended. This might be in the form of a mentor who's happy to tell all about their approach to managing a situation but also asks what you think. Or it might be a coach who helps you develop your plan but then offers to share how they've done it in the past. There are coaches who will never do this, preferring to maintain the purity of the hands-off approach. They're so focused on helping clients maximise their potential their way that intruding with their own understanding, values or experience would be regarded as highly suspect. They wouldn't say mentoring is wrong, just that it's not what they provide.

What if I do want mentoring?

If you conclude you do want a mentor rather than a coach, here are some quick tips. The rest of this book is going to focus just on coaching.

- tell a prospective coach / mentor that you've thought about this aspect of working with them, and ask how they handle the potential differences between coaching and mentoring

- be clear in advance on the kind of things you'd like to learn in a mentoring way - and any key areas where you might want coaching instead
- be careful in checking what experience and skills the mentor has. If you're going to learn how to do something their way, you want to be sure their experience is relevant to your situation and that their skills are top-notch.

Is it mostly coaching or mentoring that I want?

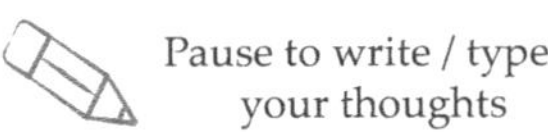

The limits of coaching

Coaching sounds amazing, right? A fix-all solution for every need? Well … no. There are some important limits for you to know about. Sorry!

You're interested in coaching and have probably already done some Googling about it. If so, you've almost definitely seen it presented in hugely glowing terms. You could be forgiven for thinking that coaches are modern day wizards, weaving magic for instant results.

I'm a coach. I have met and coached lots of coaches. I have commissioned and evaluated many many more. And I have to tell you that none of them has been that kind of heroic figure, and none of the results have been magic.

There are two reasons I want to burst the bubble of hype here. Firstly, you deserve to know that the success of coaching will depend hugely on YOU. The attitude, clarity and commitment you yourself bring will be crucial. We'll talk later about the importance of the coach's skills and approach, and they ARE important. But without your contribution they're pointless. Coaching is going to need you to be surprisingly open, challenge and change your thinking, make plans and carry them out. Progress will come from work rather than a wand.

Secondly, you should know that coaching isn't the solution for every need or ambition. It's a really useful tool, but no tool does everything you need. There are important limitations to what coaching can do for you. Some of these are so common I'll talk about them in a bit of detail. I want you to go into coaching with your eyes open and your expectations realistic.

1. Your coach is not God

> *"Don't bother with coaching, it's s**t. I went to a life coach about my family and nothing's changed. My dad's still a total t**t."*
>
> *[overheard on a bus in Norfolk, England]*

This piece of advice I overheard on a bus a couple of years ago is a brilliant illustration, not of the skills of this young woman's life coach but rather the importance of being clear about the limits of what coaching can achieve. Sometimes people go to a coach with a burning ambition they want to realise, and sometimes they're taking a problem they want addressing. In either case, we need to be realistic about what the coach can and can't do for us.

Where do you need to check your own expectations about coaching before you get started?

Your coach is not God. They are not going to be able to give you success and neither will they be able to remove a challenging situation. They're human just like you.

More than once, I've had to help a client reflect or rethink their hopes and expectations about what I can do for them. Yes, I have been privileged to help people succeed in job interviews, improve their team culture and build positive relationships with seemingly impossible people. But none of that has been achieved by me waving a magic wand to 'make it happen' for the client. I haven't given them the job / led their team through change / built their relationship. The success has come through a process of them gaining new insights, understanding themselves and others better, planning and refining plans, practising new things and being accountable for making progress. We've both worked hard, but my goal is for the client to achieve the results, not me.

Thankfully I haven't yet worked with a client who was so disappointed at my lack of godlike power that they gave up on me. But I do recommend to anyone interested in coaching to check your expectations and drop any hope that the coach will make issues go away for you. I'm not saying it wouldn't be nice if that were possible, but it just isn't.

2. Your coach is not your friend

Let me tell you a secret. As a coach, I quite like it the first time a client expresses frustration with me. I've never had it full-on - it's usually just a huff, albeit sometimes a big one. It doesn't always happen, and doesn't always need to, but it's satisfying when it does.

Am I mad? Am I cruel? Do I not realise this is how I make a living? No - I'm pleased because the frustration I've had from clients always comes from the realisation that I'm not going to tell them what to do. I'm not going to 'take their side' in a discussion about a challenging person or situation. I'm not going to hug it out. I'm their coach, not their friend.

You need friends. I need friends. Everyone needs friends. Human beings are made for relationships and community. Some of us realise it later in life than others, and perhaps some never really get it. But sharing life with friends is good for us - even science proves it.

BUT coaching is not friendship, and your coach is not your friend.

When you ask a coach 'what do YOU think?' you're going to find they reply with a question. Sometimes it'll be as direct as 'well what do YOU think' and sometimes it'll be more convoluted. Essentially, though, they're always to turn the focus back onto you, how YOU can make sense of the situation or develop a new idea to try. Your coach will never share the responsibility like a friend might. Their focus is on helping you grow your own abilities and confidence to solve your own problems and answer your own questions.

A FRIEND would...	A COACH would...
Give you the bus fare if you've spent all your money in the pub	Ask how you could avoid running out of money in future
Go to the shops for you if you're ill	Work with you on a plan to get a friend like that
Tinker with the car for you if you weren't sure how to fix it	Encourage you through the process of learning about car maintenance
Agree that your boss is a jerk for treating you strangely	Help you get a better understanding of how your boss might see the situation
Share their best interview answers / chat-up lines / jokes	Help you develop answers that are truly your own

Don't worry, you WILL get new insights, skills and solutions from coaching. I've just skipped through the feedback from my first 200 hours of coaching work, and every single client reported that they got those things. It's just they didn't get them from me telling them what I thought or what I would do if I was them.

Friendship works because you have someone who'll pull you out of the mud when you're struggling. Coaching works because you have someone who'll help you find your own way out. Friendship and coaching are different things for different needs.

I wouldn't want you to think that coaches are aloof, unfeeling creatures who take some kind of perverse pleasure from seeing people struggle. In my experience, coaches are some of the most warm and empathic people around. Their focus is resolutely on the client's welfare and they take enormous satisfaction from knowing they've helped clients.

It's just that the purpose of coaching is to help the client maximise their own potential as a resilient problem-solver. And, among other things, that requires that they don't jump in and 'rescue' the client by giving advice or saying how THEY would handle it. That's what friends do, not coaches.

3. Your coach is not your therapist

Coaching is great for all kinds of challenges or ambitions, including issues in your personal, family and social life. But please don't go to a coach for help with mental health disorders.

Life coaching exploded onto the scene about ten years ago and it is now a huge deal around the world. The International Coaching Federation reports that the number of life coaches internationally increased by 33%

from 2016 to 2020. They estimate that it's the second-fastest-growing industry in the world[6].

Other 'types' of coaching can get pretty personal too. Executive coaching, sports performance coaching and team coaching will all frequently deal with mindsets, relationships and habits that are deeply ingrained and not the kind of thing you're likely to discuss with your hairdresser or barber. Many coaches draw on frameworks and tools from the world of psychotherapy. One of the most common is cognitive behaviour therapy (CBT), and its insights into the relationships between our thoughts, feelings and actions can be a useful part of a coaching programme.

However, mental health problems like depression and anxiety are different and need handling differently. They need to be diagnosed by a doctor and while so-called 'talking therapies' are excellent, you need a clinically qualified therapist who has proper regulation and supervision.

---

[6] 2020 *ICF Global Coaching Study (2020)*. International Coaching Federation. https://coachingfederation.org/app/uploads/2020/09/FINAL_ICF_GCS2020_ExecutiveSummary.pdf

Dealing with the C word

So coaching's great, clearly? It can help us learn, grow, plan and achieve. Surely everyone loves every minute of it? Well ... no. There's one thing about coaching which is less appealing and much less talked-about. You won't find many YouTube videos which highlight it. It can stand in the way of success with coaching, and some of my clients have found it so unpalatable they've changed their goals or even stopped our work together.

The name of this elephant in the room? **CHANGE.**

This might be the most unacceptable C word you can say to someone about themselves. It's lovely to be asked about your ideas, your values, your strengths and your plans. But to be asked how you're going to CHANGE - that's a very different matter.

On one memorable occasion, a client threw down his pen and exclaimed "I brought you in to help us get out of this hole, not to *change* things". Don't worry - we worked through the shock and the organisation was out of regulatory enforcement in 6 months. But it WAS work for him to get through the shock of the C word. It honestly hadn't occurred to him until then - at least not consciously - that improving performance was going to involve a whole load of change. He knew he'd need assessments, plans and actions. But at first it was very unwelcome to see that those actions would likely include changes in attitudes, priorities, relationships, skills and behaviours - starting with him as the boss.

Now that you've come this far through the book, I hope it's a lot more obvious that, for you to get what you want from coaching, you're likely to be dealing with the C word too. It's such a common stumbling block, though, that I do recommend you spend a few moments now considering where it'll rear it's head when you're working with your coach. You might have already done this, but if not, the questions below will help you prepare a bit more.

What might I need to change, to achieve my goals?

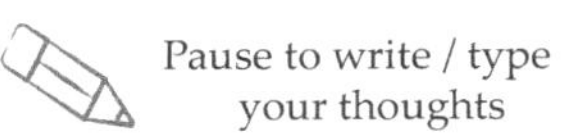

Part 2: The WHO

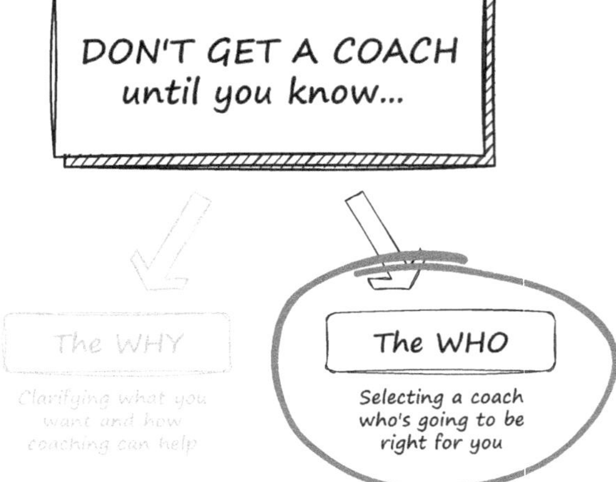

Having clarity about WHO your coach should be is the second most important foundation for success.

The WHO

Selecting a coach who's going to be right for you

We're now going to look at the second major factor for getting the most out of coaching – choosing a coach who's going to be right for you. People in the industry call this finding the right CHEMISTRY.

Whatever your reason for seeking coaching - addressing a life issue, managing a change, improving a relationship - it's going to help to feel that you have a good relationship with your coach. Even when working on strategic planning assignments with a coach, you're likely to touch on some quite personal issues. Some of the most work-related, most senior-level programmes I've undertaken with clients have involved some of the most personal development needs. So having the right chemistry is key to success as well as just being a matter of comfort.

Chemistry is so crucial that any coach worth their salt (or your time and money) will offer or even insist on having an initial 'chemistry call' with you. This is a short, free conversation in which you both have the chance to get to know each other a little, and for you both to decide if you want to work together.

Your coach will have had extensive training in doing their part of this assessment. You haven't got that sort of time, so I hope this short chapter will help you make a great decision.

It's a question of chemistry

Volumes have been written about assessing coaching relationships. This isn't that kind of book though - so here's a simple checklist of questions to help you work out if a particular coach is going to be right for you. Often, gut instinct is reliable - but you'll probably find this list is a helpful extra aid.

Here are 4 questions to ask yourself after a chemistry call with a potential coach. I suggest reading through these before a chemistry call and then making notes on each afterwards.

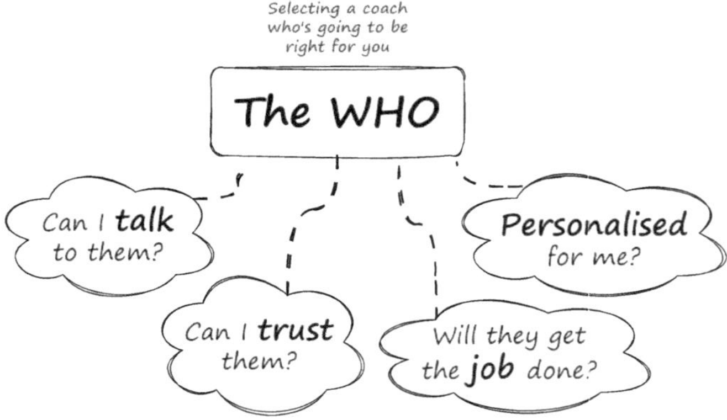

1. Is this someone I can talk to?

Do I feel comfortable talking with them? Can we go beyond a superficial 'small talk' conversation? Can I imagine being open and direct with them about my situation, my ideas and my goals?

Remember that you're not choosing a friend, so it's worth checking that you're reflecting in a different way about your chemistry conversation. You definitely want to be able to talk honestly and openly with your coach, but it's much less important whether that's an enjoyable or a sociable experience. What matters more is that your coach helps you see things differently, to focus on your goals and to provide supportive challenge as you move forward. Think of this as more like checking out a personal trainer at the gym or a teacher at your kid's school. Sure, they need to be 'nice enough' but we also want them to have a bit of the taskmaster glint in their eye.

1. Is this someone I can talk to?
(Notes after a chemistry call)

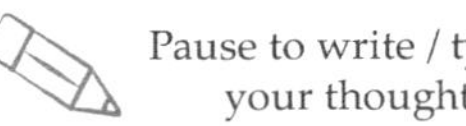

2. Is this someone I can trust?

A coach doesn't solve your problems for you or take over your work. But it's still essential that you're able to trust them, because the conversations you'll have with them will often be highly personal.

You need to be able to trust that your coach:

- will treat you with respect
- will not judge you
- will keep your appointments
- will keep your confidences
- will be accessible when you need them
- will bring great insights and ideas to the conversation
- will set and maintain boundaries in the way you want
- is active about their own professional development

You'll get a reasonable feel for some of those things from your chemistry conversation. For the rest, it's worth looking at the coach's resume or website, and reading feedback from other clients. In my experience, the quality of a coach's website says nothing about their effectiveness, but the absence of client feedback says 'run a mile'.

2. Is this someone I can trust?
(Notes after a chemistry call)

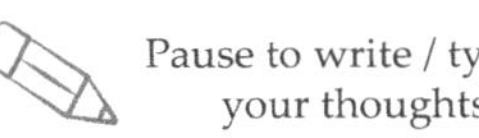

3. Will they get the job done?

Your coach is not going to be your friend, they're working with you to get a job done. As such, it's important to reflect on your chemistry conversation differently from a social conversation. We're all used to making judgements about others on the basis of how they look, how alike we are or whether we could imagine going on holiday with them. But that's not what you want to look for in a coach.

Perhaps the most important indicator of a potential coach's effectiveness is how much you felt they listened to you. Although coaching is not about providing a shoulder to cry on, it IS vital for your coach to understand your situation, your goals and your preferences. They need to listen actively, following up on what you say with further questions and demonstrating that they've both heard and understood you.

The second big thing you can listen out for here is the extent to which the potential coach is asking questions about your goals. This focus on working towards goals, making the kind of progress you want, is key to a successful coach. It's a kind of professionalism that should stand out even in your chemistry call. Above all else, they're interested in what you want to achieve and they're committed to seeing you achieve it.

3. Will they get the job done?
(Notes after a chemistry call)

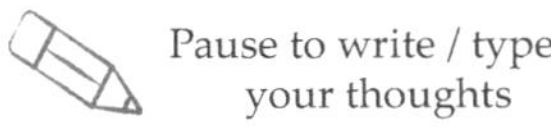

4. How will this be personalised?

One of the major advantages of coaching over other development approaches is that it can be entirely wrapped around you. Some coaches are more adaptable than others, though, so it's important to assess this aspect of their approach.

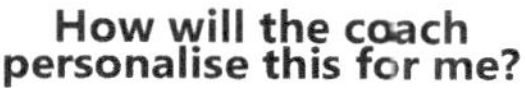

Key things to listen out for are:

- **Style.** In your chemistry call the coach will likely make some suggestions about how they could build a programme for you. Did they actively seek your feedback about that? Did they seem willing to adapt in response?
- **Scheduling.** Your coach works for you and it's entirely reasonable to select someone who's going to be available when you're available and who's prepared to be flexible for you.
- **Tools.** Coaches often draw on tools and frameworks for things like improving insights, developing plans and growing skills. I wouldn't recommend selecting a coach who doesn't have experience or qualifications in recognised tools and techniques. However, you usually don't want one who is wedded to only one approach and isn't able or willing to tailor their work to your unique situation and needs.

4. How will this be personalised?
(Notes after a chemistry call)

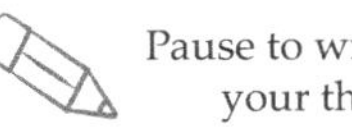

Pause to write / type your thoughts

What if the chemistry isn't right?

So what if you've had your chemistry call with a potential coach and you're not satisfied the chemistry is going to be right for you? Or what if you've already appointed a coach and you have a 'chemistry concern' after beginning to work with them?

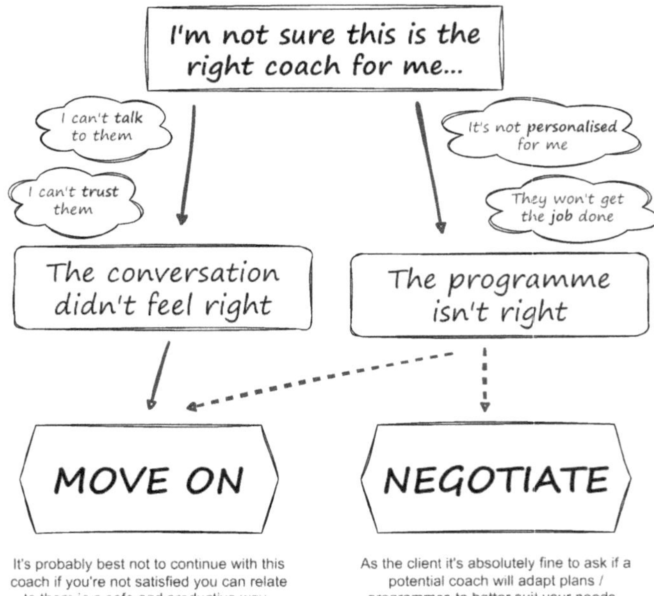

Firstly, don't panic! This is common and it's nothing to feel bad about.

Very few of us would find that every coach in the world was 'just right' and coaches know that. If you've ever bought an apartment or house, you know that it can really pay off to do some searching and not to get worried if the first viewing isn't The One.

Secondly, let's spend a few minutes getting clarity about why you're not satisfied the chemistry is right. This is going to help you decide what to do next. I recommend reviewing the chemistry questions above in this chapter and writing a few notes on each one. This should help get you a more specific answer than just "we didn't click".

My personal view is that some issues are best regarded as 'deal breakers' but that most aren't. It's often the case that an initial conversation with a potential coach throws up questions about how you'd like a programme of coaching to be structured or delivered, or the ways you'd like to be encouraged, supported or stretched. If that's the case, and you otherwise got on well with the coach as a person, I would suggest a 'negotiate' approach rather than moving on to another coach straight away. Giving the coach specific insights into how you'd like to work together will help them share back with more clarity, or help them adapt their proposed programme for you.

Ultimately, deciding whether to move on immediately or to get back to the coach with questions is one you're going to have make for yourself. I hope, though, that this makes it a little easier to get to the point where you're ready to dive in and begin a really productive programme of coaching.

What next?

I hope this little book has been helpful. Now it's over to you.

Coaching is a fantastic way to get better insights, plans and skills so you can achieve your goals. You could have just jumped in, but hopefully the ideas here and your notes will ensure you get the most out of it, by starting out with the right foundations.

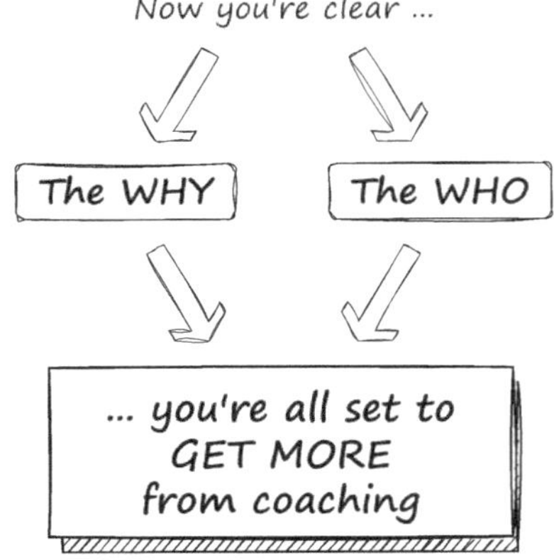

If you have comments or questions, or if you'd like to talk about booking some coaching with me, please don't hesitate to get in touch through my website.

dontgetacoach.com

Acknowledgements

This book is the result of experience and insights I have gained through working with my clients over recent years. I'm not going to name them here to protect their confidentiality, but I am truly grateful for all they have taught me about coaching and myself.

I also want to thank A and L, two of the most inspiring and challenging leaders I've ever met. Your own life and work has taught me so much, and I only started writing this book because you both had the same idea from God in the same week. Thank you! I hope you know that I'll never be able to repay your love, but I'm going to try.

I've been helped enormously by two dear friends who have, like the best coaches, brought encouragement, insights and accountability - T and J. Thank you.

Without my darling family none of this would be here, including me. I just adore you, and I thank God every time I think of you. Thank you for being you and for putting up with me.

www.ingramcontent.com/pod-product-compliance
Lightning Source LLC
LaVergne TN
LVHW052053160826
845678LV00015B/3197

* 9 7 8 1 0 6 8 5 2 4 8 0 6 *